WILD5

A Proven Path to Wellness

Saundra Jain, MA, PsyD, LPC

Rakesh Jain, MD, MPH

with Betsy Burns, PhD

ISBN 9798857629376

Dedication

This book is dedicated to those committed to leading a life filled with wellness. We applaud your dedication to creating and sustaining such a life.

This workbook is published by WILD 5 Wellness.

In an effort to make this workbook accessible to as many people as possible, the workbook is priced at the lowest level permissible. All profits from the sale of this workbook are donated to mental health charities.

Hikers follow a trail.

Stacked rocks can mark the trail and let you know you're on the right path.

When it comes to wellness, we all need a path to follow, and that's exactly what WILD 5 offers.

WILD 5 makes optimum wellness available to everyone through a proven 30-day program that combines established wellness practices and positive psychology.

After just 30 days, most people who complete the WILD 5 program increase their levels of happiness and resilience, and they lower their levels of depression, anxiety, insomnia, and chronic pain.

Table of Contents

Foreword..2

Acknowledgments...6

WILD 5 Disclaimer...7

Who created WILD 5?..8

Research behind WILD 5..10

Wellness Practices...12

Before you begin: Prepare...13

It's time to start WILD 5..15

WILD 5 Practice: Exercise...16

WILD 5 Practice: Mindfulness...22

WILD 5 Practice: Sleep..26

WILD 5 Practice: Social Connectedness...30

WILD 5 Practice: Nutrition..34

WILD 5 Practice: HERO Exercises...38

HERO Wellness Scale...41

HERO Wellness Scale–Complete on Day 1...42

Daily Tracking Sheet..43

Daily HERO Exercises..45

Reflections on Day 15..60

Plan for the Next 15 Days..61

HERO Wellness Scale–Complete on Day 30...77

Reflections and next steps..78

Congratulations on completing your WILD 5 journey...79

About the Authors..80

Reflections...81

Foreword

We suspect you have picked up this workbook in hopes of building a healthier and happier future for yourself. You will not be disappointed. The WILD 5 program has been shown in studies to improve a wide range of measures that reflect enhanced mental and physical health. In addition, we know from talking with many people who have completed the program that the benefits transcend mood and weight: increased energy, empowerment, and more positive relationships can come from this well-researched, intuitive approach to well-being.

So, it works. But if you are like us, your ability to stick with any wellness program will be enhanced by understanding the backstory of why it works. And that's where we come in. As a research psychiatrist who studies the evolved intersections of mind and body, and a behavior change expert who translates academic research to the field of personal wellness, we like the WILD 5 program because it offers a step-by-step approach to harness our ancient tendencies, so we can thrive in a modern world.

What do the most livable cities in the United States have in common? What is it about these places that situate them on the future's cutting edge? The answer is surprising: these cities don't point to the future because they reflect a science fiction vision of what's to come. They point to the future because they have begun to return to more ancient ways of living. The future these places embody is not filled with robots and flying cars, but rather is characterized by walking trails, access to fresh foods, and patterns of urban design that encourage the types of close personal connection with one's neighbors that any hunter-gatherer would recognize as normative.

We have thought many times, as we walked the streets of these cities that the buildings and sidewalks were trying to tell us something important: that the best path into a human future might first need to lead us back into the past, so that we can intelligently bring along many elements of more ancient lifeways that the first blush of modernity made us foolishly believe we could do without.

What types of ancient lifeways? The answer to this question can be seen not just in the nation's most progressive cities, but also in a range of recent cultural movements that have arisen as ways to help us cope with the stresses of the modern world. From probiotics, hot yoga, and intermittent fasting, to long distance running, neighborhood gathering spots and shopping locally, many of us crave re-exposure to ways of living that are more in keeping with how humans lived during most of our evolutionary history. We crave them not because we believe that life in the premodern world was some type of paradise, but because these ways of living make us feel healthier and happier, more grounded and less alienated — in a word, more human.

Science increasingly suggests that there is a reason these ways of life, ancient practices and patterns of association make us feel so much better than the sterile, mass produced, mechanized products we so often find ourselves surrounded by in the modern world: human beings, despite our remarkable behavioral flexibility, are not blank slates.

We evolved to function best when we get certain types of input from our social and physical environments. Some of these inputs, like feeling connected to a close group of others who know and care about us, signal that we are succeeding in the task of being human. Other types of input from our physical and social environments promote mental and physical health not because they are necessarily good in themselves, but because these inputs were constantly present across our development as a species, and so we evolved to only function optimally in their presence. As they say in evolutionary theory, what was unavoidable became necessary.

Let's consider how this applies to several core components of the WILD 5 program: healthy eating and exercise. Humans evolved in a world in which they had to eat a diverse range of natural foods to survive. We now recognize most of these foodstuffs as extremely healthy. Why are they healthy? Because they were the foods we could find and digest in ancestral environments, over time they became the foods we needed for optimal health. And finding food required effort, mental and physical. Because we had to exercise to find the foods we needed to survive, exercise became good for us. This explains, by the way, why even in the modern world exercise is more health promoting when done before, rather than after, eating.

None of us has ever seen a picture of an obese hunter-gatherer, and for good reason. The effort required to find food in the wild world of nature became balanced, again through evolutionary processes, with the amount of calories these foods delivered. But in ancestral environments where high density calories were hard to find, it became adaptive for humans to consume such foods whenever and wherever they could find them, because doing this episodically promoted survival. As long as such foods were few and far between, they were nothing but a serendipitous good.

But a key aspect of human intelligence is the ability to devise methods for shortening the path to goals that are important to us. Why put in the extra effort if there is something of great importance to us that we can get in a faster and easier way? This trait has been an incredible boon to our survival and reproduction as a species, but it has a deep and dark shadow that can be seen in most of the mental and physical health problems of the modern world, which derive from the multiple short-cuts to affluence that we've built for ourselves.

We are only now beginning as a society to understand this powerful truth: health and happiness depend as much upon the journey we take to achieve them as upon any benefit we derive from arriving at the destination. How we achieve our wants and desires, our goals and plans, is as important for our well-being as the achievements themselves.

Recognizing this is a crucial first step for attaining optimal health in the modern world, but is only a beginning. In the days before agriculture, before all the comforts and temptations of modernity, people engaged in ancient physical and social health practices not usually because they wanted to, but because they had to in order to survive. It wasn't an easy life, but calories were controlled, and strenuous exercise was necessary to get the job done.

To be clear, humans never found it easy to exercise, to eat a limited amount of food that was healthy but had none of the excessive taste to which we've grown accustomed, to endure the quirks and shortcomings of our neighbors to maintain group harmony, or to maintain the type of meditative concentration required to stalk game across the plains of Africa. But it had to be done, so we did it.

In our time, these same practices require a level of discipline that is challenging for most of us. To make these harder choices we must, at least temporarily, renounce some of the easy shortcuts the modern world provides us – not to glorify some more perfect past, but to give our evolved brains and bodies the tools we need to thrive.

Most behavior change fails because we don't set up the necessary support structures; we try to do it on our own, and we don't fully acknowledge what we'll have to give up to accomplish our goals. The WILD 5 program tackles all of these head-on, which is good because we need to marshal every advantage we can to help ourselves overcome our evolved, and ancient, tendency to always take the easiest and shortest path to the goodies.

You've already taken an important step toward change. You didn't have to sign up for this program. And you certainly didn't have to read this workbook. Research shows that many people buy self-improvement texts, get a boost from the sense of accomplishment of having made the purchase, and then never even open the book. So, congratulations. The good news is that you're already ahead of the pack.

Normally, this good news would be followed up with some bad news: even for those who read and make an honest effort to follow a behavior change technique, success is elusive. Private, individual commitments are less effective than public or group-based agreements — and reading a self-help book is a solitary act. This is where WILD 5 is different.

Working with the WILD 5 team, and joining the WILD 5 community, will dramatically increase your chances of successful behavior change. And this is re-wilding at its best: ancient practices are ones that call on us to embrace community support and open, public commitments to change. You don't have to go WILD alone.

Throughout the workbook, you'll examine what you need to give up to get what you want. This is an unpopular idea, but it's hard to deny the practical realities: if you want to add an hour of exercise into your day, what hour of other stuff are you going to give up? If you want to make more meals at home, what are you going to change about your schedule to allow for the shopping and food preparation time? Each section helps you ask those questions so that you can make decisions from the start that set you up for success.

Or, following our livable city example, let's say you are relocating to one of these progressive towns. You are excited to live in a place that has more sidewalks, local shops, community events, and farmer's markets – and you recognize that these are priorities for your well-being. Then the real estate agent looks at your budget and tells you that he can offer you a much nicer home about 15 minutes outside of town, in a suburb. The suburb is lovely, but there are no sidewalks. You'd have to drive in to town to attend community events and visit the farmer's market.

You've got a conflict, and as it is with all behavior change, the choice you make will determine how easy or difficult it will be to accomplish a whole host of other behavioral patterns. Choosing the smaller house in town will make you more likely to walk, build community with neighbors, and shop locally. Choosing the larger house outside town will likely make these practices more difficult.

The same is true with the opportunity presented to you in this WILD 5 program. Unlike most other programs that oversell one particular pathway to success, our colleagues have made available a group of practices that, when done as a group, lead you through a whole series of some of the best understood ways of tapping into ancient sources of wellness.

WILD 5 is built from a deep understanding of the brain and body connection, and how we have evolved – physically, socially, and emotionally – to thrive. By making a commitment to this program, you can set yourself up for a cascade effect of success and easier decisions in many other aspects of your life. We believe it works, and we believe you can do it.

Think of it as a journey to the most livable city around. Do your research, think about what matters most to you, and make the commitment to buy the house in the center of town. And let's go WILD... together.

Christine B. Whelan, PhD
Clinical Professor, Department of
Consumer Science

Director, Relationships, Finance & Life
Fulfillment Initiative

School of Human Ecology
University of Wisconsin-Madison

Charles L. Raison, MD
Mary Sue and Mike Shannon Chair for
Healthy Minds, Children & Families
School of Human Ecology

Professor, Department of Psychiatry
School of Medicine and Public Health
University of Wisconsin-Madison

Director of Research on Spiritual Health
Emory Healthcare
Atlanta, GA

Acknowledgments

Over the years, many people have taught us about the importance and power of wellness. We owe them all a huge debt of gratitude.

Special thanks and admiration are extended to our co-author and dear friend, Betsy Burns, PhD. Her writing genius and decades of experience as a clinical psychologist enriched this workbook in ways too numerous to mention. Her contributions elevated this workbook to new heights. We are most grateful and look forward to future projects.

A heartfelt thanks to our colleagues and friends, Charles Raison, MD and Christine Wheelan, PhD for sharing their knowledge, expertise, and wisdom regarding wellness. We've strenghthened our social connections via our many educational partnerships and hours spent talking about wellness.

A special thanks to Susan Smith, PhD, a friend and colleague, for editing the final version of the workbook and offering thoughtful feedback.

We want to recognize and thank our office manager, Jackie Smith, for her discerning eye and exceptional computer skills. She took our ideas and transformed them into extraordinary charts, documents, and tracking forms. She is not only a part of our professional family, but also part of our personal family. She reliably watches over us, always having our best interests at heart. We are forever grateful.

Finally, we extend a special thanks to each other. At times, this project required some friendly negotiating and compromises, but we did our best to remain mindful while nurturing a presence of patience and persistence. We knew this workbook would make it all worthwhile.

We hope this workbook successfully serves as a guide in your pursuit of mental wellness.

WILD 5 Disclaimer

Please talk to a healthcare provider before you start the WILD 5 program to make sure it's safe for you.

The information in this workbook cannot take the place of advice from a healthcare provider, and it is not a substitute for medical or mental health treatment.

Please make sure to:
- Follow any treatment plan you made with your healthcare provider
- Keep taking any prescribed medicines

If you notice any new or worsening physical or mental health problems after starting this program, please stop the program and contact a healthcare provider right away.

Starting the WILD 5 program does not create a professional relationship between us, and the content in this workbook is not a solicitation for healthcare-related work.

Who created WILD 5?

We are Dr. Saundra Jain and Dr. Rakesh Jain, the creators of WILD 5. We are a married couple who have more than 70 years of combined experience working in the mental health field. Saundra is a psychotherapist, and Rakesh is a psychiatrist.

Traditionally, good health has meant the absence of disease, and healthcare has focused on diagnosing and treating illness. If you weren't sick, you were considered healthy.

The World Health Organization broadened our understanding of health by saying that health is a state of complete physical, mental, and social well-being, rather than just the absence of disease. While being free of illness is good, the best state of health combines both the **absence of illness** and the **presence of wellness**.

Our interest in helping people enhance their wellness led to the creation of WILD 5. WILD is an acronym that stands for *W*ellness *I*nterventions for *L*ife's *D*emands. The 5 in WILD 5 represents the program's five wellness elements – exercise, mindfulness, sleep, social connectedness, and nutrition.

We're so excited to have you join us on this proven path to wellness. We wish you all the best as you begin your WILD 5 journey.

Saundra

Saundra Jain,
MA, PsyD, LPC

Rakesh

Rakesh Jain,
MD, MPH

Research behind WILD 5

WILD 5 is based on research.

What does the research tell us about WILD 5?

Let us show you the evidence. Everything we are sharing with you has been presented at national and international mental health meetings as research presentations and posters.

Our data show that people who completed WILD 5 reported these health improvements:

Happiness went up by **30%**

Enthusiasm went up by **51%**

Resilience went up by **63%**

Optimism went up by **45%**

Depression went down by **43%**

Anxiety went down by **40%**

Insomnia went down by **29%**

Emotional eating went down by **14%**

We set out to create a program based on sound science.

To create and test the WILD 5 program, we studied the 5 wellness practices in different settings, over 10 years, in different groups of people, such as:

- People with a mental health condition, such as depression, anxiety, or insomnia (trouble sleeping)
- People with chronic (long-lasting) pain
- People who wanted to improve their mental wellness and did not have a mental health condition or chronic pain
- People with rheumatoid arthritis
- Licensed nurses in the state of Texas who were experiencing mental health challenges or substance use disorders
- College students
- Healthcare providers wanting to elevate their wellness and experience the program firsthand

We used recognized measures from the mental health field to assess how well WILD 5 increased wellness and reduced psychological and physical symptoms.

Did we succeed in creating an effective, scientifically-based wellness program? Yes, we did. We hope that our findings will motivate you to commit to this proven path to wellness.

WILD 5 is one of only three scientifically-based wellness programs. The other two programs are Drs. Tayyab Rashid and Martin Seligman's Positive Psychotherapy and Dr. Giovanni Fava's Well-Being Therapy.

 Visit **www.WILD5Wellness.com** to learn more about the research behind WILD 5!

Wellness Practices

For 30 days, you'll complete and track daily wellness activities in these 5 areas.

Exercise 30 minutes each day for 30 days, aim for at least moderate intensity.

Practice mindfulness for at least 10 minutes each day for 30 days.

Implement 4 or more of the 6 sleep hygiene practices each day for 30 days.

Meet or call a minimum of two friends or family members each day for 30 days.

Log your daily meals, snacks, and beverages, (including alcohol) each day for 30 days.

Follow the MIND diet principles as closely as you can.

In addition to the 5 wellness practices, you'll also **answer two HERO questions each day** to enrich your levels of Happiness, Enthusiasm, Resilience, and Optimism.

Before you begin: Prepare

A little preparation goes a long way! Before you begin WILD 5, we invite you to take time to review our Tips for Success:

Tips for Success

Before you begin the program

- Consult with your healthcare provider before beginning this program.
- Review the workbook to make sure you fully understand the program before beginning.
- Make sure you have a notebook to use throughout the program.
- We invite you to do some of your wellness practices outside in nature-this can be very healing.

Get your buddies on board

- Select a wellness accountability buddy and/or a workout buddy, if you've decided to use one.
- If you wish, we invite you to inform friend(s)/family member(s) about participation in the program to gain their support and encouragement.

Get ready for Tracking

- Decide when you will complete the HERO Exercises. Consider putting these on your calendar with reminder alerts.
- Consider putting a reminder alert on your calendar to make sure you track your daily wellness practices.

Get ready for Exercise

- Make sure you have a comfortable pair of walking or running shoes.
- Review options for type of exercise and time of day for exercise. Consider putting your exercise plan on your calendar with reminder alerts.

Get ready for Mindfulness

- Review the WILD 5 Wellness Meditations. You may also consider one of the many mindfulness meditation apps currently available online. Listen to the different meditations and decide which is best, based on your needs and personal preference.
- Make these decisions prior to starting the program. Give yourself plenty of time to make this decision.
- Decide on the time and location for your mindfulness practice. Consider putting this on your calendar with reminder alerts.

Get ready for Sleep

- Consider ways to eliminate all ambient light in your bedroom, such as blackout shades and/or a sleep mask.
- Decide on your bedtime. Consider putting this on your calendar with reminder alerts.

Get ready for Social Connectedness

- Make a list of ways you want to connect with others. Consider putting these events on your calendar with reminder alerts.

Get ready for Nutrition

- If using a smartphone app to log your food and drinks, download the app and become familiar with its features.
- If you plan to follow the MIND diet, review the MIND diet recommendations, making sure your pantry's adequately stocked with brain-healthy foods.

Get ready for HERO Exercises

- Plan on setting aside 5 minutes each day to complete these exercises
- You'll need a notebook to document your answers

Your Commitment to WILD 5

Doing all of the wellness activities every day can be challenging at times. However, to get all the benefits of WILD 5, we strongly encourage you to commit to doing all of the practices daily.

Why tracking matters

Making life changes requires consistent practice, and tracking your progress helps you stay on course. It can also help you:

- Make sure you completed all daily activities
- Find patterns in your behavior
- Understand where and why you might be having difficulties

This will help you look for patterns: Do you keep forgetting a certain activity? Is there a situation that is keeping you from doing any of the WILD 5 activities? You can then problem solve, such as changing your schedule or setting reminder alerts.

It's time to start WILD 5

The workbook contains everything you'll need to complete the program.

Now, it's time to:
- Complete the HERO Wellness Scale for Day 1 (Pages 43 and 44)
- Set your start date (record below), and
- Start achieving your wellness goals

We recognize that your participation in WILD 5 requires a considerable commitment on your part, both in terms of time and in learning to incorporate new behaviors into your life. However, based on our research, the wellness benefits you'll receive from participating in the program far outweigh the sacrifices you'll be making.

Your commitment to your personal wellness begins with setting a start date.

My start date:

WILD 5 Practice

Exercise

The evidence is clear: exercise leads to positive changes in your body and brain.

Exercise can help you:

- Prevent or minimize illness, such as heart disease and diabetes
- Lower inflammation
- Strengthen muscles and joints
- Lower stress levels
- Improve sleep
- Achieve and maintain a healthy weight

Please talk to your healthcare provider before starting this exercise program to make sure it's safe for you. If you need to modify some of the practices because of a health condition, we understand. Do the best you can!

How do I kick-start my exercise program?

The goal is to follow these **FID principles.** FID stands for:

Frequency

How much?

Exercise every day

Intensity

How hard?

Aim for moderate intensity

Duration

How long?

Exercise for at least 30 minutes

Frequency

To get the full benefits of this program, exercising every day is recommended. If this seems daunting, we have some tips on how to create and stick to an exercise routine. See the section on "What might keep you from exercising every day?" on Page 22.

Intensity

Aim for moderate intensity when you exercise.

Duration

Exercise for at least 30 minutes each day. You can exercise the full 30 minutes all at once or break it into two, 15-minute-sessions or three, 10-minute-sessions. You will get the same great mind-body benefits.

How do I know if my exercise is moderate intensity?

1 **Find your target heart rate**

Your age (years)	Your target heart rate (about 65% of your maximum heart rate)		Your maximum heart rate (beats per minute)
20	130	beats per minute	200
30	124	beats per minute	190
35	120	beats per minute	185
40	117	beats per minute	180
45	114	beats per minute	175
50	111	beats per minute	170
55	107	beats per minute	165
60	104	beats per minute	160
65	101	beats per minute	155
70	98	beats per minute	150

2 **Measure your heart rate (beats per minute)**

Find your pulse

Count your heartbeat for 30 seconds

Double the number of heartbeats you count

If your heart rate is close to your target heart rate, that's moderate intensity!

Target heart rate: how many times your heart should beat to achieve moderate intensity exercise.

Maximum heart rate: how many times your heart can beat for it to still be safe.

What types of exercise do we recommend?

Here are some examples that count as moderate intensity exercise:

- Brisk walking
- Jogging
- Riding a bike
- Playing tennis
- Lifting weights
- Aerobics or water aerobics
- Swimming

Everyone has different interests and abilities, so as long as you get to your target heart rate, any activity will work. Consider mixing things up and trying more than one type of exercise.

Are there any types of exercise that don't meet the program recommendations?

People who do the WILD 5 program often ask if yoga or gardening are acceptable types of exercise. While activities like these have other great health benefits, they don't meet the FID principle of intensity. You'll get the most out of your 30 minutes of exercise if you do activities that reach a moderate intensity level.

What might keep you from exercising every day?

Here are a few challenges you might come across, and tips on how to overcome them:

Health conditions and physical limitations

You might have a health condition that stops you from following all the FID principles, such as chronic pain. If you're unable to reach 30 minutes of exercise per day or unable to reach moderate intensity, that is okay. There may be days when your health condition stops you from exercising altogether – that is okay too.

Here are some tips that might help:
- Talk to your healthcare provider about activities that are safe and healthy for you
- Take small steps to raise the duration and intensity of your exercise, such as adding a few minutes of walking per day
- Be kind to yourself on this journey – if you exercised to the best of your capabilities, you successfully completed your exercise practice for the day

Lack of time

Finding extra time in your busy schedule can be a challenge. However, it's important to make time if you want to positively impact your overall wellness. Consider these tips:
- Break down your 30 minutes of exercise into two, 15-minute sessions or three, 10-minute sessions
- Add your exercise plan to your calendar and set reminder alerts.
- Pick out your workout clothes the night before and set them out. That way, a busy morning won't get in the way of your planned exercise for the day.

Weather

If you're planning to exercise outside, it's good to have a backup plan in case weather gets in the way. If it's raining, or it's too cold or too hot, you can:
- Exercise at home
- Drive to the nearest mall for a brisk walk
- Go to your local gym or recreation center

Low motivation

Low motivation is a common feeling when starting a new exercise routine. There may be days when you don't feel like exercising. Here are some tips that might help:

- Choose a friend or family member to be your accountability buddy. Let this person know each day when you complete your workout and ask them to remind you if they don't hear from you by a certain time of day. You may even want to recruit a buddy to do WILD 5 with you.

Perfection is not the goal.
Be kind to yourself as you begin making these changes. Change can be challenging. If you miss a day or two, shake it off, regroup, and keep going!

WILD 5 Practice

Mindfulness

Mindfulness means focusing your attention on the present moment without judgment.

You may have had the experience of driving your car and arriving at your destination without remembering how you got there. Or there may be times when you realize your plate is empty, shortly after you sit down to eat, but you have no memory of eating - it's as if you're on "autopilot." When you're on autopilot, you miss out on living your life to the fullest.

Mindfulness is the opposite of this mindless, autopilot state. With mindfulness, you pay attention to your thoughts, emotions, and body without judging or analyzing them.

Research shows that mindfulness can help you:
- Lower your anxiety and stress
- Improve your mood and overall well-being
- Improve your memory and help you focus on tasks
- Strengthen your immune system
- Lower inflammation

How do I kick-start my mindfulness practice?

The goal is to practice mindfulness meditation for at least **10 minutes each day for 30 days.** You can do this in different ways:

- Listen to 1 or more of the WILD 5 Meditations at **www.WILD5Wellness.com.**
- Use a meditation app.
- If you already practice mindfulness meditation, we encourage you to continue your practice.

Tips to start your mindfulness meditation practice:

There's no right or wrong way to practice meditation

Your mind may wander frequently during some practices, and less during others. This doesn't make one practice better than another – they simply are what they are. Keep in mind that one element of mindfulness is being non-judgmental. As you begin your practice, be kind to yourself and make it a priority to practice consistently.

Decide when you will meditate

Setting aside a specific time of day can help make your practice part of your daily routine.

Minimize distractions

To ensure that you're not interrupted, let people know that you'll be unavailable during your practice. Consider leaving your phone in another room or putting it on silent.

What might keep you from meditating?

Here are a few challenges you might come across, and tips on how to overcome them:

"Beginner jitters"

If you have never meditated, and you're worried you won't do it correctly, you're not alone. Anyone can begin and grow a mindfulness meditation practice. **Remember:**

- You can use the **WILD 5 Meditations** or an online meditation app to guide you.
- Distractions during your practice are normal. Please be kind to yourself when your mind wanders. Even the Dalai Lama talks about his mind wandering during meditation.
- A mindfulness meditation practice is built through practice, patience, and self-compassion.
- There is no such thing as a 'good' or 'bad' mindfulness meditation practice.

Lack of time

Making time to practice your meditation consistently is important to get the full benefits. Regular practice creates lasting positive changes in your body and brain and works to improve your mental health. Consider these general tips:

- If time is a challenge, you can break the 10-minute-meditation into two, 5-minute blocks
- Add your practice to your calendar and set reminder alerts
- Tell your family and friends when you'll be meditating to avoid being interrupted

Low motivation

When you begin your mindfulness meditation practice, you may feel frustrated or bored. No matter what feelings you have – good, bad, or indifferent – do your best to stick with the practice and remember there is no right or wrong way to meditate.

Perfection is not the goal.
Be kind to yourself as you begin making these changes. Change can be challenging. If you miss a day or two, shake it off, regroup, and keep going!

WILD 5 Practice

Sleep

Research shows us that quality sleep is essential to our overall good health.

Getting less than 7-9 hours of sleep per night, or sleeping poorly, could negatively impact your health in the following ways:

- Getting sick more often
- Being more likely to have health problems, such as heart disease and diabetes
- Gaining weight without meaning to
- Being more likely to have mental health problems, such as depression and anxiety
- Feeling stressed and irritable
- Being unable to focus on tasks
- Having higher levels of inflammation

How do I improve the quality of my sleep?

The goal is to **use at least 4 of these 6 sleep hygiene practices** each day for 30 days:

 Turn off electronic devices 90 minutes before bedtime. Instead, wind down by listening to soothing music, meditating, or reading a book.

 Avoid napping during the day. Do your best to resist the urge to nap as this often causes poor nighttime sleep. See the next page for exceptions to this recommendation.

 Keep your bedroom as dark as possible. Try blackout shades or a night mask to block out all light.

 Enjoy a warm, relaxing bath or shower before bed.

 Establish and stick to a regular bedtime each night, including weekends.

 Avoid caffeinated drinks 10 hours before bedtime.

What might keep you from sleeping better?

Changing your sleep habits may be a challenge.

Here are some of the situations you might come across, and tips on how to overcome them.

Using electronics 90 minutes before bedtime

Many people watch TV, play video games, or scroll through their social media feed to unwind from the day. However, these electronic devices emit a blue light that can stop your body from releasing melatonin, the body's natural sleep hormone which helps regulate your sleep and wake cycles. Having too little melatonin in your body makes it hard to fall asleep.

Having to nap to meet your sleep needs

Some people may find it hard to get a full night's sleep due to life circumstances they can't control, such as shift work, young children, or illness. If that's true for you, taking a nap during the day may be necessary to meet your sleep needs. Consider these tips to help you get the most out of your nap:

- Nap around the halfway point between waking up and bedtime. For example, if you wake up at 6 a.m. and go to bed at 10 p.m., you should plan to nap around 2 p.m. Napping too late in the day will interfere with your nighttime sleep.
- Keep your naps short - no longer than 30 minutes
- Find a calm and peaceful place to nap
- Make the room as dark as possible by turning off all lights, using blackout shades, or wearing a sleep mask

Different light sources in your bedroom

Light from any source tells your body it's time to wake and be active. Light can also interfere with your body's melatonin level and lead to poor sleep. To keep your bedroom dark, try these tips:

- Use blackout shades
- Use a sleep mask
- Turn off or dim digital radios or alarm clocks, or other electronics that emit light. You can use a night light for safety if necessary.

Having caffeine within 10 hours of bedtime

It can be a challenge for some people to stop caffeine earlier in their day. Try these tips to successfully manage your caffeine consumption:

- Take your time – there is no rush
- Try decaf coffee instead of regular coffee
- Try an herbal tea, which is naturally caffeine-free

If you're used to having a lot of caffeine during the day, you may have to start lowering the amount of caffeinated drinks slowly to avoid withdrawal symptoms like headaches.

Perfection is not the goal.
Be kind to yourself as you begin making these changes.
Change can be challenging. If you miss a day or two,
shake it off, regroup, and keep going!

WILD 5 Practice

Social Connectedness

Humans are social animals – being with others is essential to our mental and physical health.

Research shows that people who socialize more often:

- Live longer
- Have fewer health problems, such as heart disease or obesity
- Have lower levels of inflammation
- Are less likely to have anxiety or depression
- Are happier overall

How do I kick-start my social connectedness?

The goal is to **meet or call at least two friends or family members** each day for 30 days.

Meeting face-to-face and spending quality time together are ideal, but when that's not possible, phone calls are great, too.

Macro- and micro-socialization

Macro-socialization means engaging in social activities with friends and family members over a period of months, years, and even a lifetime. Examples include:
- Having dinner with family or friends
- Meeting friends for coffee or a walk
- Joining a book club
- Playing sports with others, such as tennis, basketball, or racquetball
- Taking a cooking class or dance class

Micro-socialization refers to brief interactions with strangers or casual acquaintances. Examples include:
- Saying good morning to a neighbor
- Greeting people at the grocery store
- Smiling at people you pass on the street

Both macro- and micro-socialization boost your mental wellness. We invite you to practice stepping out of your comfort zone and give both a try.

Texting doesn't count.

In our research involving college students, we learned that when students used texting to fulfill the social connectedness part of the program, their connectedness scores didn't improve. Texting didn't help them feel more connected to their communities or their families. Therefore, texting does not meet the daily wellness practice of social connectedness.

What might keep you from connecting?

Here are a few challenges you might come across, and tips on how to overcome them:

Stepping out of your comfort zone

Engaging in social connectedness may mean you'll have to step out of your comfort zone, and that can be a challenge. For example, smiling at strangers on the street or talking on the phone may make some people uncomfortable. If that's true for you, we invite you to give it a try. The more you practice this, the easier it gets!

Time

Busy schedules can make it hard to find time to connect face-to-face.

Perfection is not the goal.
Be kind to yourself as you begin making these changes. Change can be challenging. If you miss a day or two, shake it off, regroup, and keep going!

WILD 5 Practice

Nutrition

We really are what we eat.

There is vast evidence to show that what we eat has a big effect on our physical and mental health. Eating a healthy, balanced diet can help you:

- Lower your chance of health problems, such as heart disease, high blood pressure, and diabetes
- Keep a healthy weight, which protects your muscles and joints
- Have lower levels of inflammation
- Have more energy and feel better overall

How do I kick-start my nutrition?

The goal is to **log everything you eat and drink** each day for 30 days in a food journal. That includes your meals, snacks, and drinks (including alcohol).

Why is a food journal helpful?

With a food journal, you simply make a list of what you eat and drink. This is a great way to be mindfully aware of what you're eating and drinking every day. By keeping track of what you take in, you're no longer engaging in "mindless eating." Mindful eating and drinking are at the heart of this practice and will help you make healthier choices.

How to keep a food journal

You may choose to use a notebook or an electronic log - either one is fine. Remember, you only need to log what you eat or drink (including alcohol). Keeping track of nutritional information, such as calories, isn't necessary unless you want to.

If you choose to keep an electronic log, there are many food journal apps online, so feel free to explore different options.

Please be aware that if you have an eating disorder or similar concerns, keeping a food journal **may not be advised.** Please consult with your healthcare provider to determine what's best for you medically. You can still participate in the WILD 5 journey without keeping a food journal.

Should I follow a certain meal plan or diet?

WILD 5 doesn't require you to follow a certain meal plan or diet. However, consider using all or some of the principles of the MIND diet:

The MIND diet

What to eat

greens
6 or more servings
per week

veggies
1 or more servings
per day

berries
2 or more servings
per week

nuts
5 or more servings
per week

olive oil
make this the
main oil you use

whole grains
3 or more servings
per day

fish
at least 1 meal
per week

beans
3 or more servings
per week

poultry
2 or more meals
per week

red wine
1 glass per day

What to limit

butter
less than 1
tablespoon per day

cheese
no more than 1
serving per week

red meat
3 or less meals
per week

fried foods
no more than 1
serving per week

sweets
4 or less servings
per week

The MIND diet was developed by
Martha Claire Morris, Ph.D. at Rush University

If you chose to follow the MIND diet, please note:

1 If you're vegan or vegetarian, you don't have to eat protein from animal sources. Simply use the parts of the MIND diet that work for you.

2 If you don't drink alcohol, are in recovery, or are underage, please disregard the recommendation to drink one glass of wine per day.

Resources to help you kick-start your nutrition

If you're new to the practice of mindful eating, we suggest you listen to Mindful Moment with a Raisin, which introduces the practice of mindful eating.

❶ Go to **WILD5Wellness.com**

❷ Click on Mindfulness in the Wellness Practices menu

❸ Scroll down to WILD 5 Meditations and play Mindful Moment with a Raisin

What might keep you from logging your nutrition choices?

Lack of time

Take the time to log your meals, snacks, and drinks (including alcohol) throughout the day instead of waiting until bedtime to complete your log. Keep up the practice, and it will get easier as you go along.

If you miss a day or two of logging your food and drinks, simply mark those days as a "No" when you do your daily tracking.

Perfection is not the goal.
Be kind to yourself as you begin making these changes. Change can be challenging. If you miss a day or two, shake it off, regroup, and keep going!

WILD 5 Practice

HERO Exercises

Many of us have external heroes. They are people we respect for their admirable qualities and abilities.

We also have an internal HERO. We've created an acronym – HERO – to represent our internal HERO traits – Happiness, Enthusiasm, Resilience, and Optimism.

It's remarkable how each of the HERO wellness traits positively impacts overall wellness. HERO is:

- Linked to longevity
- Linked to a stronger immune system
- Mitigates pain
- Predicts lower heart rate and blood pressure
- Predicts lower rates of depression
- Linked to better physical wellbeing
- Linked to better coping skills

Given these benefits, spending about 5 minutes a day strengthening your internal HERO makes sense. After completing the WILD 5 30-day program, research has shown that:

 Happiness went up by 30%   Resilience went up by 63%
Enthusiasm went up by 51%   Optimism went up by 45%

What are HERO Exercises?

In addition to the 5 daily wellness practices of exercise, mindfulness, sleep, social connectedness, and nutrition, we encourage you to answer two HERO questions, which will take about 5 minutes each day. As the data show, this practice illustrates it's possible to strengthen your internal HERO in a short period of time.

When completing your daily HERO Exercises, you can use a notebook or an electronic option, such as a journaling app or your phone or tablet.

To get the most benefit, it's important to take the time to review your previously answered HERO questions, which are recycled every eight days. We invite you to consider these questions:

❶ Are you noticing any patterns?
❷ Do you see any areas where you're struggling?
❸ Are you observing any positive changes?

This repetitive, reflective review increases your mindful awareness, which in turn strengthens your internal HERO. As you establish this daily practice, you will come to value this time of thoughtful reflection.

As you begin these exercises, you'll notice there is some overlap between the HERO wellness traits. For example, happy people are often more enthusiastic, resilient, and optimistic. Strengthening one of the HERO wellness traits helps strengthen the others.

Perfection is not the goal.
Be kind to yourself as you begin making these changes.
Change can be challenging. If you miss a day or two,
shake it off, regroup, and keep going!

HERO Wellness Scale

The HERO Wellness Scale is a tool you can use to measure your overall wellness. It asks you to rate your happiness, enthusiasm, resilience, optimism, and mental wellness for the previous 7 days, using a scale of 0-10 (0=lowest score and 10=highest score).

What does HERO stand for?

- **Happiness**: a state of well-being and contentment
- **Enthusiasm**: a strong feeling of excitement about something that you enjoy
- **Resilience**: the ability to "bounce back" when faced with adversity
- **Optimism**: expecting positive outcomes

To improve your wellness, you must measure it. You'll use the HERO Wellness Scale to measure your wellness at two points during the program:

- **The day you start the program**
- **The day you complete the program**

Please complete the HERO Wellness Scale on the next page before you begin the program. This scale is your way to measure and track your wellness throughout the program. Please don't underestimate the value of using the HERO Wellness Scale, as the feedback will be both useful and motivational.

HERO Wellness Scale - Complete on Day 1

1. On average, during the last **7 days**, how **happy** have you felt?

0	1	2	3	4	5	6	7	8	9	10

not at all happy   mildly happy   moderately happy   highly happy   extremely happy

2. On average, during the last **7 days**, how **enthusiastic** have you felt?

0	1	2	3	4	5	6	7	8	9	10

not at all enthusiastic   mildly enthusiastic   moderately enthusiastic   highly enthusiastic   extremely enthusiastic

3. On average, during the last **7 days**, how **resilient** have you felt?

0	1	2	3	4	5	6	7	8	9	10

not at all resilient   mildly resilient   moderately resilient   highly resilient   extremely resilient

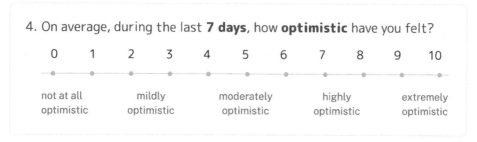

4. On average, during the last **7 days**, how **optimistic** have you felt?

0	1	2	3	4	5	6	7	8	9	10

not at all optimistic   mildly optimistic   moderately optimistic   highly optimistic   extremely optimistic

5. On average, during the last **7 days**, how would you rate your **mental wellness?**

0	1	2	3	4	5	6	7	8	9	10

not at all good   mildly good   moderately good   markedly good   extremely good

Scoring:

To calculate total score, add all circled numbers.

Possible scores range from 0-50. Higher scores indicate higher levels of wellness.

Your score

Daily Tracking

Day	Exercise Did you exercise for 30 minutes using the FID principles today?		Mindfulness Did you practice mindfulness for at least 10 minutes today?		Sleep Did you use at least 4 of the 6 sleep hygiene practices today?	
1	○Yes	○No	○Yes	○No	○Yes	○No
2	○Yes	○No	○Yes	○No	○Yes	○No
3	○Yes	○No	○Yes	○No	○Yes	○No
4	○Yes	○No	○Yes	○No	○Yes	○No
5	○Yes	○No	○Yes	○No	○Yes	○No
6	○Yes	○No	○Yes	○No	○Yes	○No
7	○Yes	○No	○Yes	○No	○Yes	○No
8	○Yes	○No	○Yes	○No	○Yes	○No
9	○Yes	○No	○Yes	○No	○Yes	○No
10	○Yes	○No	○Yes	○No	○Yes	○No
11	○Yes	○No	○Yes	○No	○Yes	○No
12	○Yes	○No	○Yes	○No	○Yes	○No
13	○Yes	○No	○Yes	○No	○Yes	○No
14	○Yes	○No	○Yes	○No	○Yes	○No
15	○Yes	○No	○Yes	○No	○Yes	○No
16	○Yes	○No	○Yes	○No	○Yes	○No
17	○Yes	○No	○Yes	○No	○Yes	○No
18	○Yes	○No	○Yes	○No	○Yes	○No
19	○Yes	○No	○Yes	○No	○Yes	○No
20	○Yes	○No	○Yes	○No	○Yes	○No
21	○Yes	○No	○Yes	○No	○Yes	○No
22	○Yes	○No	○Yes	○No	○Yes	○No
23	○Yes	○No	○Yes	○No	○Yes	○No
24	○Yes	○No	○Yes	○No	○Yes	○No
25	○Yes	○No	○Yes	○No	○Yes	○No
26	○Yes	○No	○Yes	○No	○Yes	○No
27	○Yes	○No	○Yes	○No	○Yes	○No
28	○Yes	○No	○Yes	○No	○Yes	○No
29	○Yes	○No	○Yes	○No	○Yes	○No
30	○Yes	○No	○Yes	○No	○Yes	○No

Social Connectedness

Did you meet or call at least 2 friends or family members today?

○ Yes	○ No
○ Yes	○ No
○ Yes	○ No
○ Yes	○ No
○ Yes	○ No
○ Yes	○ No
○ Yes	○ No
○ Yes	○ No
○ Yes	○ No
○ Yes	○ No
○ Yes	○ No
○ Yes	○ No
○ Yes	○ No
○ Yes	○ No
○ Yes	○ No
○ Yes	○ No
○ Yes	○ No
○ Yes	○ No
○ Yes	○ No
○ Yes	○ No
○ Yes	○ No
○ Yes	○ No
○ Yes	○ No
○ Yes	○ No
○ Yes	○ No
○ Yes	○ No
○ Yes	○ No
○ Yes	○ No
○ Yes	○ No
○ Yes	○ No

Nutrition

Did you track your daily meals, snacks, and drinks (including alcohol) today?

○ Yes	○ No
○ Yes	○ No
○ Yes	○ No
○ Yes	○ No
○ Yes	○ No
○ Yes	○ No
○ Yes	○ No
○ Yes	○ No
○ Yes	○ No
○ Yes	○ No
○ Yes	○ No
○ Yes	○ No
○ Yes	○ No
○ Yes	○ No
○ Yes	○ No
○ Yes	○ No
○ Yes	○ No
○ Yes	○ No
○ Yes	○ No
○ Yes	○ No
○ Yes	○ No
○ Yes	○ No
○ Yes	○ No
○ Yes	○ No
○ Yes	○ No
○ Yes	○ No
○ Yes	○ No
○ Yes	○ No
○ Yes	○ No
○ Yes	○ No

HERO Exercises

Did you complete your HERO Exercises today?

○ Yes	○ No
○ Yes	○ No
○ Yes	○ No
○ Yes	○ No
○ Yes	○ No
○ Yes	○ No
○ Yes	○ No
○ Yes	○ No
○ Yes	○ No
○ Yes	○ No
○ Yes	○ No
○ Yes	○ No
○ Yes	○ No
○ Yes	○ No
○ Yes	○ No
○ Yes	○ No
○ Yes	○ No
○ Yes	○ No
○ Yes	○ No
○ Yes	○ No
○ Yes	○ No
○ Yes	○ No
○ Yes	○ No
○ Yes	○ No
○ Yes	○ No
○ Yes	○ No
○ Yes	○ No
○ Yes	○ No
○ Yes	○ No
○ Yes	○ No

HERO Exercises - Day 1
Happiness and enthusiasm are linked to longevity.

1 **To increase your happiness, let's work on strengthening your happiness muscle.**

Take a moment and write down two positive things that you'd like to experience today. Also, two to three times today, find a few minutes to visualize and relish these positive experiences.

_____

_____

_____

_____

_____

2 **Having a goal or a project that inspires you will increase your enthusiasm.**

Write down two projects you find inspiring and set a start date. Put the date on your calendar with reminder alerts – make it happen and watch your enthusiasm improve!

_____

_____

_____

_____

_____

"Enthusiasm moves the world."

~ Arthur Balfour

HERO Exercises are designed to improve your mental wellness. Doing them daily increases and enriches your levels of Happiness, Enthusiasm, Resilience, and Optimism.

The HERO Exercises repeat every 8 days because repetition is crucial to learning new ideas and using them in your life.

After today, we invite you to review your past HERO Exercises in your notebook. Research shows that reflecting on past thoughts about wellness further strengthens and solidifies your HERO wellness traits.

HERO Exercises - Day 2

Resilient optimists have better physical health and better relationships.

1 **Resilience means the ability to bounce back from adversities.**

Write down 2 things about yourself that make you tough, and two skills you have used previously to overcome adversities. Remind yourself throughout the day that you genuinely possess these resilient traits.

_____

_____

_____

_____

_____

2 **Optimism often requires making a choice about how you view the world.**

Write down two positive things you want to happen tomorrow, and then spend a few minutes planning on how to make these optimistic attitudes/events a reality.

_____

_____

_____

_____

_____

"Choose to be optimistic; it feels better."

~ Dalai Lama XIV

HERO Exercises are designed to improve your mental wellness. Doing them daily increases and enriches your levels of Happiness, Enthusiasm, Resilience, and Optimism.

The HERO Exercises repeat every 8 days because repetition is crucial to learning new ideas and using them in your life.

We invite you to review your past HERO Exercises in your notebook. Research shows that reflecting on past thoughts about wellness further strengthens and solidifies your HERO wellness traits.

HERO Exercises - Day 3
Happiness and enthusiasm are linked to a stronger immune system.

1 **In today's busy world, it's easy to overlook things that make us happy.**

Fast-paced lifestyles often become a barrier. Take a moment and mindfully reflect on your day and write down two things that brought you happiness.

_____

_____

_____

_____

_____

2 **"Birds of a feather flock together," so surround yourself with happy and enthusiastic people.**

Write down the names of two people in your life that are happy and enthusiastic. Now, write down how and when you will connect with them.

_____

_____

_____

_____

_____

"Enthusiasm is contagious. You want to be a carrier."

~ Susan Rabin

HERO Exercises are designed to improve your mental wellness. Doing them daily increases and enriches your levels of Happiness, Enthusiasm, Resilience, and Optimism.

The HERO Exercises repeat every 8 days because repetition is crucial to learning new ideas and using them in your life.

We invite you to review your past HERO Exercises in your notebook. Research shows that reflecting on past thoughts about wellness further strengthens and solidifies your HERO wellness traits.

HERO Exercises - Day 4
Resilient and optimistic people report better mental health & live longer.

1 **Dealing with life's challenges with humor builds resilience – the ability to bounce back from life's adversities.**

Write down two things that happened recently that you found humorous – things that made you smile or laugh.

_____

_____

_____

_____

_____

2 **Positive affirmations are a great way to build an optimistic mindset.**

Take a moment and write down two positive statements about yourself, your life, or your future. Purposefully remind yourself of these affirmations several times throughout your day.

_____

_____

_____

_____

_____

"Our greatest ally in life is our resilience."

~ Brian Early

HERO Exercises are designed to improve your mental wellness. Doing them daily increases and enriches your levels of Happiness, Enthusiasm, Resilience, and Optimism.

The HERO Exercises repeat every 8 days because repetition is crucial to learning new ideas and using them in your life.

We invite you to review your past HERO Exercises in your notebook. Research shows that reflecting on past thoughts about wellness further strengthens and solidifies your HERO wellness traits.

1 **Random acts of kindness will increase your happiness!**

Take a moment and write down two random acts of kindness you will put into action today. If you don't have time to execute your plan today, be sure to make it happen first thing tomorrow morning.

_____

_____

_____

_____

_____

2 **When it comes to outlook, do you fall on the positive or the negative side of the fence?**

Having a positive attitude about life improves enthusiasm. To increase your enthusiasm, mindfully consider your day and write down two examples of your positive attitude and/or actions.

_____

_____

_____

_____

"Most folks are as happy as they make up their minds to be."

~ Abraham Lincoln

HERO Exercises are designed to improve your mental wellness. Doing them daily increases and enriches your levels of Happiness, Enthusiasm, Resilience, and Optimism.

The HERO Exercises repeat every 8 days because repetition is crucial to learning new ideas and using them in your life.

We invite you to review your past HERO Exercises in your notebook. Research shows that reflecting on past thoughts about wellness further strengthens and solidifies your HERO wellness traits.

HERO Exercises - Day 6
Resilience and optimism fertilize a positive attitude.

1

Being of service to others is a great way to build resilience.

List two things you did today (or will do tomorrow) to give back to others or to brighten their day.

_____

_____

_____

_____

_____

2

Is your glass half-full or half-empty? How you view the world matters!

Write down two things that happened today that you viewed as negative. Take a moment and give this some thought, and then write down a less negative, or even a positive interpretation of the same events.

_____

_____

_____

_____

_____

"In order to carry a positive action, we must develop here a positive vision."

~ Dalai Lama

HERO Exercises are designed to improve your mental wellness. Doing them daily increases and enriches your levels of Happiness, Enthusiasm, Resilience, and Optimism.

The HERO Exercises repeat every 8 days because repetition is crucial to learning new ideas and using them in your life.

We invite you to review your past HERO Exercises in your notebook. Research shows that reflecting on past thoughts about wellness further strengthens and solidifies your HERO wellness traits.

HERO Exercises - Day 7

Happiness and enthusiasm predict lower heart rate and blood pressure.

1 **Thinking about happy memories can positively impact your level of happiness!**

Write down two memories that bring a smile to your face. Next, spend a few minutes reliving each of these happy memories, and watch your current level of happiness increase.

_____

_____

_____

_____

2 **Gratitude is known to increase feelings of happiness and enthusiasm.**

To increase these feelings, mindfully consider your day and write down two examples of things that happened today that increased your feelings of gratitude.

_____

_____

_____

_____

> "The worst bankruptcy in the world is the person who has lost his enthusiasm."
>
> ~ H.W. Arnold

HERO Exercises are designed to improve your mental wellness. Doing them daily increases and enriches your levels of Happiness, Enthusiasm, Resilience, and Optimism.

The HERO Exercises repeat every 8 days because repetition is crucial to learning new ideas and using them in your life.

We invite you to review your past HERO Exercises in your notebook. Research shows that reflecting on past thoughts about wellness further strengthens and solidifies your HERO wellness traits.

HERO Exercises - Day 8

Resilience and optimism are linked to greater life satisfaction.

1 **People are quick to point out faults and weaknesses. Acknowledging others' successes is a great way to build and strengthen your resilience while making another person feel great.**

Think of two people that have recently achieved some type of success, personal or work-related, and write down how you plan to acknowledge their achievement.

_____

_____

_____

_____

2 **Have you heard of Paying it Forward? Someone does something kind for you and you pass it forward by doing something kind for another.**

Write down two times others have done something kind for you and how that made you feel. Make a plan to pass along those acts of kindness and brighten someone else's day.

_____

_____

_____

"Our greatest glory is not in never falling, but in rising every time we fall."

~ Confucius

HERO Exercises are designed to improve your mental wellness. Doing them daily increases and enriches your levels of Happiness, Enthusiasm, Resilience, and Optimism.

The HERO Exercises repeat every 8 days because repetition is crucial to learning new ideas and using them in your life.

We invite you to review your past HERO Exercises in your notebook. Research shows that reflecting on past thoughts about wellness further strengthens and solidifies your HERO wellness traits.

HERO Exercises - Day 9

Happiness and enthusiasm are linked to longevity.

1 **To increase your happiness, let's work on strengthening your happiness muscle.**

Take a moment and write down two positive things that you'd like to experience today. Also, two to three times today, find a few minutes to visualize and relish these positive experiences.

_____

_____

_____

_____

_____

_____

2 **Having a goal or a project that inspires you will increase your enthusiasm.**

Write down two projects you find inspiring and set a start date. Put the date on your calendar with reminder alerts – make it happen and watch your enthusiasm improve!

_____

_____

_____

_____

_____

_____

"The real secret to success is enthusiasm."

~ Walter Chrysler

HERO Exercises are designed to improve your mental wellness. Doing them daily increases and enriches your levels of Happiness, Enthusiasm, Resilience, and Optimism.

The HERO Exercises repeat every 8 days because repetition is crucial to learning new ideas and using them in your life.

We invite you to review your past HERO Exercises in your notebook. Research shows that reflecting on past thoughts about wellness further strengthens and solidifies your HERO wellness traits.

HERO Exercises - Day 10
Resilient optimists have better physical health and better relationships.

1 **Resilience means the ability to bounce back from adversities.**

Write down 2 things about yourself that make you tough, and two skills you have used previously to overcome adversities. Remind yourself throughout the day that you genuinely possess these resilient traits.

_____

_____

_____

_____

_____

2 **Optimism often requires making a choice about how you view the world.**

Write down two positive things you want to happen tomorrow, and then spend a few minutes planning on how to make these optimistic attitudes/events a reality.

_____

_____

_____

_____

_____

"Happiness is not something readymade. It comes from your own actions."

~ Dalai Lama

HERO Exercises are designed to improve your mental wellness. Doing them daily increases and enriches your levels of Happiness, Enthusiasm, Resilience, and Optimism.

The HERO Exercises repeat every 8 days because repetition is crucial to learning new ideas and using them in your life.

We invite you to review your past HERO Exercises in your notebook. Research shows that reflecting on past thoughts about wellness further strengthens and solidifies your HERO wellness traits.

HERO Exercises - Day 11
Happiness and enthusiasm are linked to a stronger immune system.

1 **In today's busy world, it's easy to overlook things that make us happy.**

Fast-paced lifestyles often become a barrier. Take a moment and mindfully reflect on your day and write down two things that brought you happiness.

_____

_____

_____

_____

_____

2 **"Birds of a feather flock together," so surround yourself with happy and enthusiastic people.**

Write down the names of two people in your life that are happy and enthusiastic. Now, write down how and when you will connect with them.

_____

_____

_____

_____

_____

"It is not how much we have, but how much we enjoy,
that makes happiness."

~ Charles Spurgeon

HERO Exercises are designed to improve your mental wellness. Doing them daily increases and enriches your levels of Happiness, Enthusiasm, Resilience, and Optimism.

The HERO Exercises repeat every 8 days because repetition is crucial to learning new ideas and using them in your life.

We invite you to review your past HERO Exercises in your notebook. Research shows that reflecting on past thoughts about wellness further strengthens and solidifies your HERO wellness traits.

HERO Exercises - Day 12
Resilient and optimistic people report better mental health & live longer.

1 **Dealing with life's challenges with humor builds resilience – the ability to bounce back from life's adversities.**

Write down two things that happened recently that you found humorous – things that made you smile or laugh.

_____

_____

_____

_____

_____

2 **Positive affirmations are a great way to build an optimistic mindset.**

Take a moment and write down two positive statements about yourself, your life, or your future. Purposefully remind yourself of these affirmations several times throughout your day.

_____

_____

_____

_____

_____

"Although the world is full of suffering, it is also full of the overcoming of it."

~ Helen Keller

HERO Exercises are designed to improve your mental wellness. Doing them daily increases and enriches your levels of Happiness, Enthusiasm, Resilience, and Optimism.

The HERO Exercises repeat every 8 days because repetition is crucial to learning new ideas and using them in your life.

We invite you to review your past HERO Exercises in your notebook. Research shows that reflecting on past thoughts about wellness further strengthens and solidifies your HERO wellness traits.

HERO Exercises - Day 13
Happiness and enthusiasm are known to lessen pain.

1 **Random acts of kindness will increase your happiness!**

Take a moment and write down two random acts of kindness you will put into action today. If you don't have time to execute your plan today, be sure to make it happen first thing tomorrow morning.

_____

_____

_____

_____

_____

2 **When it comes to outlook, do you fall on the positive or the negative side of the fence?**

Having a positive attitude about life improves enthusiasm. To increase your enthusiasm, mindfully consider your day and write down two examples of your positive attitude and/or actions.

_____

_____

_____

_____

_____

"Love is the master key that opens the gates of happiness."

~ Oliver Wendell Holmes

HERO Exercises are designed to improve your mental wellness. Doing them daily increases and enriches your levels of Happiness, Enthusiasm, Resilience, and Optimism.

The HERO Exercises repeat every 8 days because repetition is crucial to learning new ideas and using them in your life.

We invite you to review your past HERO Exercises in your notebook. Research shows that reflecting on past thoughts about wellness further strengthens and solidifies your HERO wellness traits.

HERO Exercises - Day 14
Resilience and optimism fertilize a positive attitude.

1 **Being of service to others is a great way to build resilience.**

List two things you did today (or will do tomorrow) to give back to others or to brighten their day.

_____

_____

_____

_____

_____

2 **Is your glass half-full or half-empty? How you view the world matters!**

Write down two things that happened today that you viewed as negative. Take a moment and give this some thought, and then write down a less negative, or even a positive interpretation of the same events.

_____

_____

_____

_____

_____

"Man never made any material as resilient as the human spirit."

~ Bern Williams

HERO Exercises are designed to improve your mental wellness. Doing them daily increases and enriches your levels of Happiness, Enthusiasm, Resilience, and Optimism.

The HERO Exercises repeat every 8 days because repetition is crucial to learning new ideas and using them in your life.

We invite you to review your past HERO Exercises in your notebook. Research shows that reflecting on past thoughts about wellness further strengthens and solidifies your HERO wellness traits.

HERO Exercises - Day 15
Happiness and enthusiasm predict lower heart rate and blood pressure.

1 **Thinking about happy memories can positively impact your level of happiness!**

Write down two memories that bring a smile to your face. Next, spend a few minutes reliving each of these happy memories, and watch your current level of happiness increase.

_____

_____

_____

_____

_____

2 **Gratitude is known to increase feelings of happiness and enthusiasm.**

To increase these feelings, mindfully consider your day and write down two examples of things that happened today that increased your feelings of gratitude.

_____

_____

_____

_____

"None are so old as those who have outlived enthusiasm."

~ Henry David Thoreau

HERO Exercises are designed to improve your mental wellness. Doing them daily increases and enriches your levels of Happiness, Enthusiasm, Resilience, and Optimism.

The HERO Exercises repeat every 8 days because repetition is crucial to learning new ideas and using them in your life.

We invite you to review your past HERO Exercises in your notebook. Research shows that reflecting on past thoughts about wellness further strengthens and solidifies your HERO wellness traits.

Reflections on Day 15

This halfway point offers an opportunity to reflect on your first 15 days, allowing you to make minor adjustments regarding any challenges you may have encountered. No matter what your experiences have been during the first 15 days - positive, negative, or mixed - we strongly encourage you to take the time to complete this section. We believe your reflections will uncover useful information that may improve the final 15 days of your WILD 5 experience.

Respond to these questions:

What did I learn about myself during the first 15 days of WILD 5?

_____

_____

_____

What challenges have I encountered during the first 15 days of WILD 5?

_____

_____

_____

What changes and adjustments have I made to overcome these challenges?

_____

_____

_____

Plan for the Next 15 Days

Now that you have reviewed the first 15 days of your wellness program, take a moment to answer the questions below. The goal is to identify ways to improve your WILD 5 experience during the next 15 days.

What can I do to increase the chances that I will successfully complete the WILD 5 program?

_____

_____

_____

To successfully complete the program, what changes or adjustments will I make to overcome the challenges I encountered?

_____

_____

_____

What are 3 ways I can improve my WILD 5 experience?

_____

_____

_____

Perfection is not the goal.
Be kind to yourself as you begin making these changes. Change can be challenging. If you miss a day or two, shake it off, regroup, and keep going.

HERO Exercises - Day 16
Resilience and optimism are linked to greater life satisfaction.

1 **People are quick to point out faults and weaknesses. Acknowledging others' successes is a great way to build and strengthen your resilience while making another person feel great.**

Think of two people that have recently achieved some type of success, personal or work-related, and write down how you plan to acknowledge their achievement.

_____

_____

_____

_____

_____

2 **Have you heard of Paying it Forward? Someone does something kind for you and you pass it forward by doing something kind for another.**

Write down two times others have done something kind for you and how that made you feel. Make a plan to pass along those acts of kindness and brighten someone else's day.

_____

_____

_____

_____

_____

"Perpetual optimism is a force multiplier."

~ Colin Powell

HERO Exercises are designed to improve your mental wellness. Doing them daily increases and enriches your levels of Happiness, Enthusiasm, Resilience, and Optimism.

The HERO Exercises repeat every 8 days because repetition is crucial to learning new ideas and using them in your life.

We invite you to review your past HERO Exercises in your notebook. Research shows that reflecting on past thoughts about wellness further strengthens and solidifies your HERO wellness traits.

HERO Exercises - Day 17
Happiness and enthusiasm are linked to longevity.

1 **To increase your happiness, let's work on strengthening your happiness muscle.**

Take a moment and write down two positive things that you'd like to experience today. Also, two to three times today, find a few minutes to visualize and relish these positive experiences.

_____

_____

_____

_____

_____

2 **Having a goal or a project that inspires you will increase your enthusiasm.**

Write down two projects you find inspiring and set a start date. Put the date on your calendar with reminder alerts – make it happen and watch your enthusiasm improve!

_____

_____

_____

_____

_____

"Enthusiasm is the steam that drives the engine."

~ Napoleon Hill

HERO Exercises are designed to improve your mental wellness. Doing them daily increases and enriches your levels of Happiness, Enthusiasm, Resilience, and Optimism.

The HERO Exercises repeat every 8 days because repetition is crucial to learning new ideas and using them in your life.

We invite you to review your past HERO Exercises in your notebook. Research shows that reflecting on past thoughts about wellness further strengthens and solidifies your HERO wellness traits.

HERO Exercises - Day 18
Resilient optimists have better physical health and better relationships.

1 **Resilience means the ability to bounce back from adversities.**

Write down 2 things about yourself that make you tough, and two skills you have used previously to overcome adversities. Remind yourself throughout the day that you genuinely possess these resilient traits.

_____

_____

_____

_____

2 **Optimism often requires making a choice about how you view the world.**

Write down two positive things you want to happen tomorrow, and then spend a few minutes planning on how to make these optimistic attitudes/events a reality.

_____

_____

_____

_____

"It does not matter how slowly you go so long as you do not stop."

~ Andy Warhol

HERO Exercises are designed to improve your mental wellness. Doing them daily increases and enriches your levels of Happiness, Enthusiasm, Resilience, and Optimism.

The HERO Exercises repeat every 8 days because repetition is crucial to learning new ideas and using them in your life.

We invite you to review your past HERO Exercises in your notebook. Research shows that reflecting on past thoughts about wellness further strengthens and solidifies your HERO wellness traits.

HERO Exercises - Day 19
Happiness and enthusiasm are linked to a stronger immune system.

1 **In today's busy world, it's easy to overlook things that make us happy.**

Fast-paced lifestyles often become a barrier. Take a moment and mindfully reflect on your day and write down two things that brought you happiness.

_____

_____

_____

_____

_____

2 **"Birds of a feather flock together," so surround yourself with happy and enthusiastic people.**

Write down the names of two people in your life that are happy and enthusiastic. Now, write down how and when you will connect with them.

_____

_____

_____

_____

_____

"Learn to let go. That is the key to happiness."

~ Buddha

HERO Exercises are designed to improve your mental wellness. Doing them daily increases and enriches your levels of Happiness, Enthusiasm, Resilience, and Optimism.

The HERO Exercises repeat every 8 days because repetition is crucial to learning new ideas and using them in your life.

We invite you to review your past HERO Exercises in your notebook. Research shows that reflecting on past thoughts about wellness further strengthens and solidifies your HERO wellness traits.

HERO Exercises - Day 20

Resilient and optimistic people report better mental health & live longer.

1 **Dealing with life's challenges with humor builds resilience – the ability to bounce back from life's adversities.**

Write down two things that happened recently that you found humorous – things that made you smile or laugh.

_____

_____

_____

_____

_____

2 **Positive affirmations are a great way to build an optimistic mindset.**

Take a moment and write down two positive statements about yourself, your life, or your future. Purposefully remind yourself of these affirmations several times throughout your day.

_____

_____

_____

_____

_____

"Don't leave home without it...YOU were born
with Bounce-Back Ability!"

~ Ty Howard

HERO Exercises are designed to improve your mental wellness. Doing them daily increases and enriches your levels of Happiness, Enthusiasm, Resilience, and Optimism.

The HERO Exercises repeat every 8 days because repetition is crucial to learning new ideas and using them in your life.

We invite you to review your past HERO Exercises in your notebook. Research shows that reflecting on past thoughts about wellness further strengthens and solidifies your HERO wellness traits.

HERO Exercises - Day 21
Happiness and enthusiasm are known to lessen pain.

1 **Random acts of kindness will increase your happiness!**

Take a moment and write down two random acts of kindness you will put into action today. If you don't have time to execute your plan today, be sure to make it happen first thing tomorrow morning.

_____

_____

_____

_____

_____

2 **When it comes to outlook, do you fall on the positive or the negative side of the fence?**

Having a positive attitude about life improves enthusiasm. To increase your enthusiasm, mindfully consider your day and write down two examples of your positive attitude and/or actions.

_____

_____

_____

_____

_____

"Most smiles are started by another smile."

~ Frank A. Clark

HERO Exercises are designed to improve your mental wellness. Doing them daily increases and enriches your levels of Happiness, Enthusiasm, Resilience, and Optimism.

The HERO Exercises repeat every 8 days because repetition is crucial to learning new ideas and using them in your life.

We invite you to review your past HERO Exercises in your notebook. Research shows that reflecting on past thoughts about wellness further strengthens and solidifies your HERO wellness traits.

HERO Exercises - Day 22
Resilience and optimism fertilize a positive attitude.

1 **Being of service to others is a great way to build resilience.**

List two things you did today (or will do tomorrow) to give back to others or to brighten their day.

_____

_____

_____

_____

_____

2 **Is your glass half-full or half-empty? How you view the world matters!**

Write down two things that happened today that you viewed as negative. Take a moment and give this some thought, and then write down a less negative, or even a positive interpretation of the same events.

_____

_____

_____

_____

_____

"I have not failed. I've just found 10,000 ways that won't work."

~ Thomas A. Edison

HERO Exercises are designed to improve your mental wellness. Doing them daily increases and enriches your levels of Happiness, Enthusiasm, Resilience, and Optimism.

The HERO Exercises repeat every 8 days because repetition is crucial to learning new ideas and using them in your life.

We invite you to review your past HERO Exercises in your notebook. Research shows that reflecting on past thoughts about wellness further strengthens and solidifies your HERO wellness traits.

HERO Exercises - Day 23

Happiness and enthusiasm predict lower heart rate and blood pressure.

1 **Thinking about happy memories can positively impact your level of happiness!**

Write down two memories that bring a smile to your face. Next, spend a few minutes reliving each of these happy memories, and watch your current level of happiness increase.

_____

_____

_____

_____

_____

_____

2 **Gratitude is known to increase feelings of happiness and enthusiasm.**

To increase these feelings, mindfully consider your day and write down two examples of things that happened today that increased your feelings of gratitude.

_____

_____

_____

_____

"I have chosen to be HAPPY because it's good for my HEALTH."

~ Voltaire

HERO Exercises are designed to improve your mental wellness. Doing them daily increases and enriches your levels of Happiness, Enthusiasm, Resilience, and Optimism.

The HERO Exercises repeat every 8 days because repetition is crucial to learning new ideas and using them in your life.

We invite you to review your past HERO Exercises in your notebook. Research shows that reflecting on past thoughts about wellness further strengthens and solidifies your HERO wellness traits.

HERO Exercises - Day 24
Resilience and optimism are linked to greater life satisfaction.

1 **People are quick to point out faults and weaknesses. Acknowledging others' successes is a great way to build and strengthen your resilience while making another person feel great.**

Think of two people that have recently achieved some type of success, personal or work-related, and write down how you plan to acknowledge their achievement.

_____

_____

_____

_____

_____

_____

2 **Have you heard of Paying it Forward? Someone does something kind for you and you pass it forward by doing something kind for another.**

Write down two times others have done something kind for you and how that made you feel. Make a plan to pass along those acts of kindness and brighten someone else's day.

_____

_____

_____

_____

"Optimism is the best way to see life."

~ Anonymous

HERO Exercises are designed to improve your mental wellness. Doing them daily increases and enriches your levels of Happiness, Enthusiasm, Resilience, and Optimism.

The HERO Exercises repeat every 8 days because repetition is crucial to learning new ideas and using them in your life.

We invite you to review your past HERO Exercises in your notebook. Research shows that reflecting on past thoughts about wellness further strengthens and solidifies your HERO wellness traits.

1 **To increase your happiness, let's work on strengthening your happiness muscle.**

Take a moment and write down two positive things that you'd like to experience today. Also, two to three times today, find a few minutes to visualize and relish these positive experiences.

_____

_____

_____

_____

_____

2 **Having a goal or a project that inspires you will increase your enthusiasm.**

Write down two projects you find inspiring and set a start date. Put the date on your calendar with reminder alerts – make it happen and watch your enthusiasm improve!

_____

_____

_____

_____

_____

"Happiness is the synonym of well-being."

~ Bruce Lee

HERO Exercises are designed to improve your mental wellness. Doing them daily increases and enriches your levels of Happiness, Enthusiasm, Resilience, and Optimism.

The HERO Exercises repeat every 8 days because repetition is crucial to learning new ideas and using them in your life.

We invite you to review your past HERO Exercises in your notebook. Research shows that reflecting on past thoughts about wellness further strengthens and solidifies your HERO wellness traits.

HERO Exercises - Day 26
Resilient optimists have better physical health and better relationships.

1 **Resilience means the ability to bounce back from adversities.**

Write down 2 things about yourself that make you tough, and two skills you have used previously to overcome adversities. Remind yourself throughout the day that you genuinely possess these resilient traits.

_____

_____

_____

_____

_____

2 **Optimism often requires making a choice about how you view the world.**

Write down two positive things you want to happen tomorrow, and then spend a few minutes planning on how to make these optimistic attitudes/events a reality.

_____

_____

_____

_____

_____

"Optimism is the faith that leads to achievement."

~ Helen Keller

HERO Exercises are designed to improve your mental wellness. Doing them daily increases and enriches your levels of Happiness, Enthusiasm, Resilience, and Optimism.

The HERO Exercises repeat every 8 days because repetition is crucial to learning new ideas and using them in your life.

We invite you to review your past HERO Exercises in your notebook. Research shows that reflecting on past thoughts about wellness further strengthens and solidifies your HERO wellness traits.

HERO Exercises - Day 27

Happiness and enthusiasm are linked to a stronger immune system.

1 **In today's busy world, it's easy to overlook things that make us happy.**

Fast-paced lifestyles often become a barrier. Take a moment and mindfully reflect on your day and write down two things that brought you happiness.

_____

_____

_____

_____

_____

2 **"Birds of a feather flock together," so surround yourself with happy and enthusiastic people.**

Write down the names of two people in your life that are happy and enthusiastic. Now, write down how and when you will connect with them.

_____

_____

_____

_____

_____

"If you aren't fired with enthusiasm, you'll be fired with enthusiasm."

~ Vincent Lombardi

HERO Exercises are designed to improve your mental wellness. Doing them daily increases and enriches your levels of Happiness, Enthusiasm, Resilience, and Optimism.

The HERO Exercises repeat every 8 days because repetition is crucial to learning new ideas and using them in your life.

We invite you to review your past HERO Exercises in your notebook. Research shows that reflecting on past thoughts about wellness further strengthens and solidifies your HERO wellness traits.

HERO Exercises - Day 28
Resilient and optimistic people report better mental health & live longer.

1 **Dealing with life's challenges with humor builds resilience – the ability to bounce back from life's adversities.**

Write down two things that happened recently that you found humorous – things that made you smile or laugh.

_____

_____

_____

_____

_____

2 **Positive affirmations are a great way to build an optimistic mindset.**

Take a moment and write down two positive statements about yourself, your life, or your future. Purposefully remind yourself of these affirmations several times throughout your day.

_____

_____

_____

_____

_____

"Real optimism has reason to complain but prefers to smile."

~ William Arthur Ward

HERO Exercises are designed to improve your mental wellness. Doing them daily increases and enriches your levels of Happiness, Enthusiasm, Resilience, and Optimism.

The HERO Exercises repeat every 8 days because repetition is crucial to learning new ideas and using them in your life.

We invite you to review your past HERO Exercises in your notebook. Research shows that reflecting on past thoughts about wellness further strengthens and solidifies your HERO wellness traits.

HERO Exercises - Day 29
Happiness and enthusiasm are known to lessen pain.

1 **Random acts of kindness will increase your happiness!**

Take a moment and write down two random acts of kindness you will put into action today. If you don't have time to execute your plan today, be sure to make it happen first thing tomorrow morning.

_____

_____

_____

_____

_____

2 **When it comes to outlook, do you fall on the positive or the negative side of the fence?**

Having a positive attitude about life improves enthusiasm. To increase your enthusiasm, mindfully consider your day and write down two examples of your positive attitude and/or actions.

_____

_____

_____

_____

_____

"Happiness is talking to a friend that makes you feel
that everything's going to be ok."

~ Anonymous

HERO Exercises are designed to improve your mental wellness. Doing them daily increases and enriches your levels of Happiness, Enthusiasm, Resilience, and Optimism.

The HERO Exercises repeat every 8 days because repetition is crucial to learning new ideas and using them in your life.

We invite you to review your past HERO Exercises in your notebook. Research shows that reflecting on past thoughts about wellness further strengthens and solidifies your HERO wellness traits.

HERO Exercises - Day 30
Resilience and optimism fertilize a positive attitude.

1 **Being of service to others is a great way to build resilience.**

List two things you did today (or will do tomorrow) to give back to others or to brighten their day.

_____

_____

_____

_____

2 **Is your glass half-full or half-empty? How you view the world matters!**

Write down two things that happened today that you viewed as negative. Take a moment and give this some thought, and then write down a less negative, or even a positive interpretation of the same events.

_____

_____

_____

_____

"It comes down to perseverance and resiliency."

~ Roger Staubach

Now, complete the HERO Wellness Scale on the next page.

Please don't underestimate the value of using the HERO Wellness Scale, as the feedback will be both useful and motivational. →

HERO Wellness Scale - Complete on Day 30

1. On average, during the last **7 days**, how **happy** have you felt?

0	1	2	3	4	5	6	7	8	9	10

not at all happy   mildly happy   moderately happy   highly happy   extremely happy

2. On average, during the last **7 days**, how **enthusiastic** have you felt?

0	1	2	3	4	5	6	7	8	9	10

not at all enthusiastic   mildly enthusiastic   moderately enthusiastic   highly enthusiastic   extremely enthusiastic

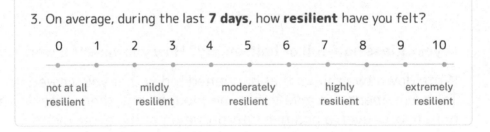

3. On average, during the last **7 days**, how **resilient** have you felt?

0	1	2	3	4	5	6	7	8	9	10

not at all resilient   mildly resilient   moderately resilient   highly resilient   extremely resilient

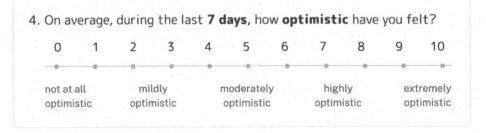

4. On average, during the last **7 days**, how **optimistic** have you felt?

0	1	2	3	4	5	6	7	8	9	10

not at all optimistic   mildly optimistic   moderately optimistic   highly optimistic   extremely optimistic

5. On average, during the last **7 days**, how would you rate your **mental wellness?**

0	1	2	3	4	5	6	7	8	9	10

not at all good   mildly good   moderately good   markedly good   extremely good

Scoring:

To calculate total score, add all circled numbers.

Possible scores range from 0-50. Higher scores indicate higher levels of wellness.

Your score

Reflections and next steps

We encourage you to document your Day 1 and Day 30 HERO Wellness Scale scores below. Your scores will offer some insight into how your wellness changed throughout WILD 5.

HERO Wellness Scale

Day 1: _____   Day 30: _____

Finally, we encourage you to take a moment to write about your WILD 5 experiences. You might want to consider the following questions:

- What did you learn about yourself during this 30-day wellness experience?
- How has your wellness improved?
- Was WILD 5 worth the time and effort?
- Will you continue these wellness practices?

_____

_____

_____

_____

_____

_____

_____

_____

_____

_____

_____

Congratulations on Completing Your WILD 5 Journey

We're very proud of you for taking such a big step toward your mental and physical wellness.

Please don't stop here! Nurture your newfound wellness practices by continuing this proven path to wellness. Most people find that consistently doing these practices 3 days a week helps them sustain the benefits of WILD 5.

 Visit **www.WILD5Wellness.com** for an interactive, online WILD 5 experience!

Our best to you as you continue on this proven path to wellness.

Be Well,

Saundra and Rakesh

About the Authors

Saundra Jain, MA, PsyD, LPC, is a seasoned psychotherapist, educator, and strong supporter of living a life based on wellness practices. Years of clinical practice and dealing with life's ups and downs have convinced her that wellness practices of exercise, mindfulness meditation, optimized sleep, social connectedness, and a nutritious diet are all essential wellness elements. She is the co-creator of WILD 5 Wellness.

Rakesh Jain, MD, MPH, is an experienced psychiatrist, researcher, and educator who firmly believes that life is much more than not having symptoms of mental illness. He believes that the attainment of mental wellness is our ultimate goal. Years of experience have taught him that mental wellness is a highly learnable skill and can be strengthened with practice. According to Dr. Jain, the purpose of WILD 5 Wellness is to help people deal with life's daily stresses and to flourish. He is the co-creator of WILD 5 Wellness.

Betsy Burns, PhD, is a clinical psychologist who has a personal and professional interest in wellness. For most of her career, she has worked with acutely ill, hospitalized psychiatric patients. In the last several years, her focus has broadened to include working with people who are interested in learning how to increase their overall sense of wellbeing.

Reflections

Reflections

Made in the USA
Columbia, SC
14 January 2025

51805980R00050